To Olivia

The Business Of Nonprofit-*ing*

*Best wishes in all your
endeavors!*

Amy Fass

Amy Fass

Olivia, This book was given to us for you by Tom's property manager, Lisa Esslin. It is signed by the author, Amey Fass and meant to be given to you —

Lisa has been invaluable to Tom for over 5 years.

The Business Of Nonprofit-*ing*

Amy Fass

Live Your Dreams Out Loud Media Inc

This book is dedicated to Shoes That Fit's partners
who are working to make the world better for
our children, and to Richard and Allegra
who make my world a better place.

If you don't like the way the world is you change it.
You just do it one step at a time.

—Marian Wright Edelman

CONTENTS

Running a business is difficult. Running a non-profit business is a whole different animal that requires a different tool kit to achieve excellence. I have worked with Amy for many years in her executive role at Shoes that Fit. More than anyone, she understands the challenges of running a nonprofit and she excels in achieving the very best outcomes for her team and her organization. She has the tool kit that works.

—Cara Esposito, Executive Director,
Leonetti/O'Connell Family Foundation;
Adjunct Professor, Sol Price School of Business,
University of Southern California

When I first met Amy she changed my perspective on the business of nonprofits with a single conversation that has stayed with me for many years. I was beyond thrilled when she told me about this book. Amy is a transformational leader that leads from the front and brings a depth and breadth of insights and experience that make this book not just timely but immediately applicable to nonprofit organizations everywhere.

—Tony Kopetchny, CEO,
Parsons TKO

Amy Fass is a force–a force that has had an incredible impact of the lives of children experiencing poverty. I am so proud to have partnered with Amy to serve youth and families who truly need us most. Amy's understanding of the intricacies associated with nonprofits and the benefits of partnership make her a phenomenal leader.

Her collaborative style is quite impressive, but more than anything I love that Amy continues to learn and lean on others for advice and authentic perspective on the communities she serves. She doesn't turn a blind eye to what is needed but rather pivots to ensure her approach and that of her organization are community driven and sensitive to the needs of her beneficiaries.

—Nichol Whiteman, CEO,
Los Angeles Dodgers Foundation

Amy Fass headed the corporate and foundation relations program at Pomona College when I was president there. Both gracious and ambitious, she was not only visionary but also results-oriented. No one better understood how or was more successful explaining to others why supporting the College was an investment in the future. Ultimately, her sense of mission led her beyond a career as an all-star fundraiser toward broader forms of leadership in the not-for-profit world. Our loss was society's gain.

—Peter W. Stanley, President
Emeritus, Pomona College

I have observed Amy in three nonprofit settings over 25 years: fundraising peer at Pomona College, management consultant for the American Museum of Ceramic Art, and CEO of Shoes That Fit. She is a consummate fundraiser as well as an extraordinary leader—inspirational, visionary, pragmatic—someone who enhances the effectiveness and achievements of individuals and transforms the fortunes of nonprofits.

—Don Pattison, Senior Philanthropy Advisor,
Pomona College (retired), and past President,
American Museum of Ceramic Art

Strong, innovative leaders will surround themselves with the people and resources they need to complement their strengths and talents. Over the past few years, I have seen Amy seek executive coaching and leadership development programs, as well as actively invite guidance from her fellow executive directors. She has an open mind and a growth mindset, important qualities for an ED to lead change and growth in their organization. Amy is a gift to the nonprofit sector and we all have so much to learn from her!

—Janet McIntyre, Vice President of Programs and Training, Executive Service Corps

I've had the opportunity to work with Amy since she joined Shoes That Fit in 2014. It's impressive and inspiring to see the passion she brings to her role, which is such an essential ingredient to successfully lead a non-profit organization. Whether working with her team, the board, donors, schools or business partners, Amy's authenticity and ability to bring the story and mission of Shoes That Fit to life has created an incredible community of support. It's through years of experience that Amy has built her leadership style and gained the insights to write this book. I know it will be a fantastic resource for any non-profit organization.

—Scott Meden, Chief Marketing Officer, Nordstrom Inc.

Intelligent. Brave. Strategic. Thoughtful. Kind. And overall good human being. There's so much that I can say about Amy Fass. What's most important, is that she is a wonderful human being who is utilizing her gift of gab to improve the Nonprofit space through her thought leadership. What she's doing at STF is simply remarkable and should be taught in a classroom one day. Thank you Amy for giving me a front row seat to see this story unfold. The world needs more Amy's but I'm glad that I know this one.

—Brian Johnson, TV Host & Entrepreneur

Chapter 1

Who, Me?

Life is what happens when you are busy making other plans.

—John Lennon

I dreamed of becoming many things as a child, but being the CEO of a nonprofit was never one of them. I would guess that MOST of us in the nonprofit industry never dreamed about this world growing up. There is no one route people take that leads to running a nonprofit. My own path was far from linear, and I know many of my colleagues have similar stories. But when I tell my story, I think my path has been more meandering than average.

As a child, I made several moves that affected my view of myself and the world. I was born in Washington DC and grew up in Baltimore. I spent most of my childhood summers in Iowa, moved to Dallas in high school, moved to California for college, and eventually settled down in Southern California. I feel lucky that I have seen our country from many different angles. But I also know what it feels like to not fit in.

I feel lucky that I have seen our country from many different angles. But I also know what it feels like to not fit in.

In the 1960s and 70s, before the inner harbor was revitalized, Baltimore was a tough city, with high rates of poverty and deep racial segregation. I remember driving through derelict row houses to get to school and feeling guilty. We were far from rich, but compared to the poverty I saw as a matter of course not far from my house, I knew that I was lucky—and at some level, I knew that it was not fair. This discomfort has been a theme in my life.

Most of my neighborhood friends went to local Catholic schools, while I went to a small school that was part of our Lutheran church. My school ended at 6th grade, so I transferred to Friends School, a private school north of downtown Baltimore. Friends was an incredibly important chapter of my life, but the first year was difficult; most of my classmates had been together since kindergarten, and they lived on the other side of town, which meant I didn't see them much outside of school. All in all, I ended up living in three worlds–my church friends, my neighborhood friends, and "Friends friends." My worlds never really integrated. This also became a theme for me.

During the summer, we would visit my mother's large family in Iowa. My grandfather had been a Missouri Synod Lutheran missionary in Brazil when he and my grandmother first married; when he returned ten years later with his four oldest surviving children in tow, he founded a Lutheran church in rural Homestead, Iowa. I loved seeing my aunts and uncles and cousins, of which there were many! But I always felt like we were the outsiders—most of the rest of the family saw each other all the time. Even more than that, we were from the East Coast and we more "urbanites." The fact that my father rarely came with us emphasized the difference.

Later in life, I learned that I come from a long line of German Lutheran pastors, which skipped a generation and somehow landed on my head. I went to seminary. If you know anything about the Missouri Synod, you will understand that having a granddaughter go to seminary did not please my grandfather, nor most of my relatives. I didn't really understand that growing up. As a child, I was a people-pleaser and felt the Church was a noble calling.

Actually, what I wanted to be growing up was a U.S. senator. To be president felt like too much pressure, and it sounded isolating, especially lacking any examples of women in the role. But the Senate looked like a team sport—a group of people working together on issues to make the country stronger. My dad had worked for the Security and Exchange Commission when I was little, and I grew up surrounded by politics. Being a senator meant working as part of group of leaders to make the country better. It was that simple. When I was older, I began to realize how difficult politics could be. But I never let go of the desire to be part of a group working together to make the world better. This is a third theme that informed many decisions in my life.

At the end of my freshman year in high school, we moved to Highland Park in Dallas, Texas. This was not a family decision—my father took a new job and announced the move. The culture shock that I experienced from moving to Dallas was on par with studying abroad in Italy later in life. We were a somewhat mid-western, somewhat preppy, deeply fractured, East Coast family that moved into a wealthy area of Dallas. Even more so than at Friends, the kids had all truly grown up together, and Texas pride was high. Football was everything—there was no lacrosse, field hockey or basketball for girls, which was how I spent much of my free time at Friends. I had never worn make-up. You can probably picture it—I did not fit in at all. So my work the next three years was to figure out how to become an "insider."

Because of my upbringing and background, I learned to be a chameleon. This was a survival skill that I learned very early on. While my younger brothers were more rebellious, I always wanted to be part of the group. I learned that people can be quite judgmental of "outsiders," but I could usually find a way to adapt. On my college application to Stanford, I had to identify one word to describe myself, and I chose "sensitive"—I tend to be thin-skinned and hard on myself, but I am also highly attuned to how others are feeling and have a strong inner compass when I perceive others to be treated unfairly. I am often more at home with "outsiders" and those who struggle to fit in. Between my own life experiences and being an adult child of an alcoholic, I tend to see things through multiple perspectives. This can be exhausting.

One thing I'll say for Texas is that people there have some of the best (and often most colorful) sayings. One that has stuck with me my whole life is "God can't move a parked car." Because I am sensitive and at times overly-analytical, with a tendency to see situations from multiple perspectives, decisions could be paralyzing. Sometimes you just have to start moving and trust that you will figure it out as you go! I have referenced that saying frequently in my life, especially when I have a tough decision to make.

Apart from being a senator, which I let go of after moving to Texas (where no one was going to elect an outsider like me!), I wanted to be a professional singer. Singing was a huge part of my life growing up—it was an emotional release, and I found in high school that I was really quite good! I started out as a music major at Stanford (again, much to my family's horror—for someone who was a people pleaser, I really did upend their expectations whenever I could!). There was just one problem: I was terrified of speaking in front of people, much less performing a solo.

My freshman year, I studied voice with an opera singer, Vera Scammon, who was a visiting professor at Stanford for just one year. She invited me to join her in Vienna to study opera for the following year. It was an amazing opportunity. But my fear of performing—of really putting myself out there—held me back. I let my fears win. I later swore I would never do that again. After that, I put myself in more and more positions where I either had to speak or sing in front of others. If I had not learned how to perform publicly, I could never have taken this job, which has led me to speak on TV, in front of large groups, and with famous celebrities and athletes—this is something I would have never dreamed I could do when I was 18. One of the most important lessons in life is that half the battle is just showing up.

After graduating from Stanford, I knew I wanted to be in a field helping people. I spent a few years doing college ministry, which I loved, and teaching. People I respected urged me to go into ministry full-time, and the church needed more women in positions of leadership. It felt like going to seminary was something I should do, so I went.

I never felt completely at home while I was there. I was elected president of the student body and was a teacher's assistant for the school's provost and incoming president, but I always felt like an outsider. The questions I was asking were not the questions the rest of the student body were asking, and I did not agree with many of the answers I heard. As the tension between fitting-in or speaking-out became more exhausting, I began to leave behind other people's opinions. Slowly, I came to realize that my rationale for attending seminary had little to do with what I actually wanted in life. I was doing what others wanted me to do. It was time to change.

I decided to transition into higher education and began applying to different schools. I took a job as director of Foundation and Corporate Relations at Pomona College, which was my introduction to development and a turning point in my career. I lacked the experience Pomona was looking for, but after a failed job search, the person who had been promoted out of the position gave my application a second look. In her words, I had "made a persuasive case out of nothing." To my surprise, I got the job.

My first day at Pomona was the same day that the new college dean's tenure began. This was also serendipitous because my job required me to work closely with the dean. One of my early assignments with her was to write a proposal to a foundation promoting discourses in liberal-arts colleges about diversity and values. The request for proposals, although a noble cause, amounted to a large sum of money with very vague goals. And unfortunately, the dean provided little guidance or ideas to get me started.

I turned to a faculty member in the Philosophy Department to help me put together some ideas based on conversations the faculty were having. I sent a rough outline to the dean but did not receive a response. As the deadline approached, I was a nervous wreck, but eventually, I finalized a draft that I delivered to both the president and the dean. Surprisingly, the president signed it without much red ink (a rarity as he was a superb academic and writer), and we submitted on the Friday it was due, with little time to spare. Close to 5pm., I heard someone shout my name from other end of the long hallway. It was the dean, and she did not sound happy. Marching from her office at one corner of the building toward my office at the other end, she was holding the signed proposal and shouted "Amy, this is a piece of S#*T! How could you submit this?" She then stomped back down to her office with the rest of the development office watching. I was humiliated.

My first reaction was fear—had I really screwed up? I was shocked that she would yell at me like that in front of everyone…and then I was furious. I simply could not go through the weekend stewing about this; with encouragement from colleagues who watched the whole unfortunate scene, I collected my teary-eyed self and walked down to her office. "That was extremely unfair," I began. "You gave me nothing to work with. I asked for your input time and again, which you ignored. The president liked the proposal and signed it. It's been submitted. So you're going to have to live with it—but if we don't get the grant, don't blame me." Having said my piece, I walked out. I assumed I would be fired.

To my surprise, Pomona did not fire me. A few weeks later, we were awarded the grant. In fact, the Foundation used our proposal as an example of what they were looking for. When I arrived at my office before I heard the news, I found a can of Coke with a little black bird standing on top with a note: "Dean eats crow." I cannot tell you what that human and humorous connection meant to me. (In the dean's defense, she was not completely wrong—the program we put in place was NOT the great solution imagined and caused more problems than it solved. But that's another story.)

At Pomona, I learned to build a case for support. Gradually, I not only understood the basics of how to craft a compelling proposal and to create a plan to drive growth, but I also began to understand myself. I found a home at Pomona, and I developed friendships and mentors like the president of the college, as well as faculty, staff and donors.

Fundraising is an amorphous concept, which I learned through the process of doing it over and over again at Pomona. The basic question we had to answer was: "You are a wealthy college—why should I fund you?" In many ways, that's what ministry is—listening to people, discovering what matters to them, and helping reframe. I took to it.

Overall, I discovered that fundraising is about two basic things: listening and presenting a case of what can be. In many ways, that's what ministry is— listening to people, discovering what matters to them, and helping reframe. I took to it.

Overall, I discovered that fundraising is about two basic things: listening and presenting a case of what can be.

One of the hardest professional decisions I made was leaving a job at a place I loved. I had met my husband at Pomona. The genteel nature of Pomona meant that fundraising was never rushed and relationships ran deep. I knew I was leaving a prestigious institution where I was set up to be a success with people who believed in me. I was newly married, with a long daily commute to downtown Los Angeles, but now I would be in a much more high-pressured environment working in major gifts for the University of California, Berkeley's unprecedented $1.2 billion campaign. I knew I had a lot to learn, and there was a chance I would not be as successful as I had been at Pomona. But I decided not to live in fear. I took the chance.

The first few months were rough, and I was sure I'd made a mistake. These heart-versus-head moments often seem so uncertain. I was introduced to a completely different way of working. The decision to work for the University of California, Berkeley (or Cal), as it turned out, was one of the best decisions I could make. My office in Pomona and the people I surrounded myself with there were my family, but I don't think I would be where I am today without taking that calculated risk. The much larger operation at Cal offered new opportunities, the challenge of a $1.2 billion campaign, and my introduction to soliciting major donations.

The organization moved quickly—often just attending an event led to a solicitation in the weeks following. I recall writing a strategy for a $100,000 solicitation; I was going to take the vice chancellor to meet a donor he had never met and I had only spoken with on the phone. (This would never have happened at Pomona!) I was proud of myself for crafting a bold ask; the donor said yes immediately. That's never a good sign, and I later learned that I had significantly undershot the dollar amount for the solicitation. It turned out that he and his wife were prepared to donate $1,000,000 to the campaign, which they eventually did. Through the experience, I learned that I enjoyed fundraising with individuals—at a basic level, I saw that people wanted to make a difference. My job was to help them do that.

After my daughter was born, I did not want to be on the road as much, so I decided to stop working for a while. Those were wonderful years. But I have to confess that I was always nervous about how I was going to get back into my career. The first way I tried to keep myself "fresh" was by consulting, primarily with smaller nonprofits that were looking for help with fundraising. In fact, Shoes That Fit was one of the first organizations I consulted for. Beyond my professional experience in fundraising, I found that the most useful experiences I brought to these consulting experiences—not to mention my current job—were my experiences as a board member with a variety of nonprofits and agencies. No two organizations were similar, starting with Claremont Heritage (historical preservation organization), House of Ruth (domestic violence agency), Mt. San Antonio Gardens (retirement community) and even our City's Architectural Commission. I chaired each of these boards—twice during capital campaigns, twice during executive searches, and one for seven years during a period of intense growth and change. I was always surprised at how deeply involved I became with each of these organizations and how much I learned from being able to see situations from different sides of the table, as both a staff member and from the board's perspective.

Reflecting on my professional experiences, my career has been everything but linear. I originally said no when the former executive director asked if I would take over Shoes That Fit when she retired. I fully intended to go back into higher education and

And being a parent continues to remind me how much there always is to learn and that our kids are everything. They are our future.

had never envisioned myself leading a nonprofit. It took me a while to come to the obvious realization that nonprofits have been exactly where I have spent the majority of my adult life—whether in the church, in higher education, as a board member or as a consultant. I have gained a significant amount of experience throughout the years. It has not always been experience I wanted, and I never dreamed it would fit together.

Baltimore formed me and showed me the extremes of wealth and poverty juxtaposed in this country—and often racial disparities—from an early age. My Iowa relatives were hard-working, generous people who taught me humility even when our politics differed. Dallas taught me how to package material, and how to use humor and pithy quotes to make people comfortable. Stanford and Friends taught me how to think critically. Seminary taught me how to stand up for myself and break free of others' perceptions of me. Pomona taught me how to make a case and fundraise and how to learn to be confident in my own skin, while Berkeley taught me to think big and bold. And being

22

a parent continues to remind me how much there always is to learn, and most importantly, that our kids are everything. They are our future. They deserve the best we can give them.

In the end, leading Shoes That Fit has become the perfect "fit" for me. At its core, Shoes That Fit is investing in children's dignity. Our secret sauce is that we are not about shoes—we are about kids. Shoes are an often overlooked need. There's enough goodness and enough money in this world, and there's no need for children to suffer and feel humiliated.

I feel lucky to have the job I have and to love what I do. But I believe the nonprofit world is misunderstood. That is why I decided to write this book, to explain the *Business of Nonprofit-ing*.

Chapter 2

The Story of Shoes That Fit

Every great dream begins with a dreamer. Always remember,
you have within you the strength, the patience, and the passion
to reach for the stars to change the world.

—Harriet Tubman

Shoes That Fit is a direct and concrete response to the overwhelming problem of child poverty in the United States. We tackle one of the most visible signs of poverty in America by giving children in need new athletic shoes to attend school with dignity and joy, so they are prepared to learn, play and thrive. Our mission is much larger than shoes—we remove a basic barrier to a child's success and invest in their self-esteem, providing an often overlooked item that is intrinsically important to a child's sense of self. Our organization is a piece of the puzzle in addressing an enormous problem.

Children are disproportionately affected by poverty. The poverty threshold in early 2021 was $26,500 or less for a family of four. While approximately 7.7% of our population live at or below the poverty line (currently defined as an income of $26,500 for a family of four), over 16% of our children live in poverty. Shoes are one of the most expensive items low-income families have to provide their growing children. When trying to decide whether to feed your children or buy them new shoes, there is no question that food will win. That is where we step in.

There is a huge impact on children who do not have shoes or are wearing inappropriate shoes. To start with, shoes are required to go to school. In many districts you can't attend physical education classes or go on field trips without appropriate close-toed shoes. I remember chaperoning my daughter's second-grade class on a field trip when one little boy was told he could not go because of his flip flops. (The teachers eventually found something for him, but it was an awful situation for him and his family.)

Shoes are cool. Kids really care about shoes. Everyone knows the feeling of walking in brand-new shoes. It puts a smile on your face. You stand up taller. That experience alone can do so much for your sense of self and how you feel about life. Kids look up to athletes and popular culture mentors who are associated with shoe brands. At a basic level, a pair of shoes helps a child who wants to fit in; giving children shoes increases self-esteem on a fundamental level. Children who wear shoes that belong to a relative—that smell or are falling apart—face embarrassment and shame. It affects attendance and leads to behavioral issues. Shoes are fundamental to a child's sense of self-worth. Giving a child a pair of good shoes is a simple, concrete action that anyone can do to make a difference in a child's life today.

Shoes That Fit provides new, high-quality athletic shoes that kids are proud to wear. We have amazing volunteer programs across the country, where people work closely with schools in their own communities and understand what kids want. As an organization, we focus on high-quality, name-brand shoes. We want kids to have what they want and need. We provide shoes kids can be proud to wear. And we evaluate our program by the impact it has on the children we serve.

The unique way that Shoes That Fit carries out its mission is important —almost as important as the shoes themselves. We could increase our service volume if we filled a big rig with low-quality shoes, parked it in Pershing Square in Los Angeles, and let people take whatever they wanted. That would distribute shoes quickly.

27

But our mission is not about shoes—it is about children and providing something they need in a way that affirms their dignity. We work with schools and teachers in low-income communities to identify the children most in need. We

The unique way that Shoes That Fit carries out its mission is important— almost as important as the shoes themselves.

provide the size that the child needs and the shoes are given to the child in private. Over the years, we have received countless thank-you notes from children who think their teachers purchased their shoes. (In reality, there are teachers across the country who ARE purchasing shoes and other necessities for children in their classes! Bless them!) When schools are in very high-need communities, we often work with donors who want to provide shoes for the entire school--then it's a party! We do not talk about need or circumstances with the children. We focus on providing kids with something they deserve. Because they do deserve good shoes—these kids are our future.

I am often asked for stories about kids who have been helped by Shoes That Fit, and there are two that I return to; these stories ground me on difficult days. The first is from the organization's early days. A young boy in Pomona had a truancy problem. His parents dropped him off at school, but he would often disappear before going in. One day, the principal found him hiding in the bushes. He noticed the boy was wearing his sister's shoes—they were pink plastic "jelly" sandals. He had been teased and bullied, so not surprisingly, he hated school. The school called us to help, and we were able to get him a new pair of sneakers that day. The principal later told us that, after getting his shoes, the boy didn't miss another day of school that year. We still have that pair of pink jelly shoes in our office as a kind of talisman.

Another story is from one of the first deliveries I attended as executive director. It was a large delivery event with one of our corporate partners. I saw a little girl sitting to the side, hugging her shoebox. The other kids were trying on their shoes, showing each other and running around, but she did not budge. I found her teacher, and we went to talk with her and asked if she liked her shoes and if she wanted help trying them on. She shook her head and said quietly, I've never had a new box like this." That response never

"I've never had a new box like this."

occurred to me. I still tear up when I think about her. Teachers and school administrators are our most important partners and our biggest fans. They know their students and which families are struggling. And they are the ones who tell us about the concrete impact shoes have on a child's school attendance, behavior, attitude, level of activity on the playground and interactions with

87% of teachers reported improvement in self-esteem among the children who received new shoes.

classmates. But year after year, the number one improvement that schools report is in a child's self-esteem. Last year, 87% of teachers responding to our survey reported improvement in self-esteem among the children who received new shoes, 80% reported improvement in attitude, and 40% reported an increase in attendance.

Early on in the pandemic, when most children attended school remotely from their homes, schools continued to function as resource hubs in many low-income communities. The Los Angeles Unified School District (LAUSD) is the nation's second largest district, with more than 80% of its students living in poverty. This past year, LAUSD provided more than 100 million meals to families in their communities who have been struggling. Many low-income districts provided hot spots, laptops and tablets, homework packets, and materials that students

Teachers would tell us that a call from us was often the first piece of good news they had received since the pandemic began.

needed. We continued to work through many of these schools; the teachers would tell us that a call from us was often the first piece of good news they had received since the pandemic began. They would report how meaningful it was to children stuck at home, or for families that were struggling, to know that the community cared about them The following words of this school principal speak to the power of new shoes:

"You may think that a new pair of shoes does little to help students academically. But let me be the first to tell you that when a child feels safe and happy—if they are not inhibited by their physical environment—only then can real learning occur. The new shoes your organization provided help students to not feel embarrassed anymore because of torn, dirty, and ill-fitting shoes."

—Principal Stayman, Paul E. Culley Elementary, Las Vegas

I am the third executive director of Shoes That Fit. Our amazing founder, Elodie (Silva) McGuirk, was a single mom who responded to a story about a little boy whose toes had literally been turned under to make them fit into his shoes. The story haunted her; she started a movement. Her successor, Roni Lomeli, took a growing organization and launched two major national partnerships, first with Rack Room Shoes and then with Nordstrom. I owe a great deal to them for the wonderful organization they created.

When I was first approached about the job, I saw Shoes That Fit as a local organization with a nice mission, but not as something I wanted to seriously consider as a career move. I have already told you that I never saw myself running a nonprofit. What I did not tell you is that shoes are NOT my thing. I wear a size 11 shoe. My feet are not my favorite asset...they are not even in my top 10 list of things I like about myself. What I had to come to see is that Shoes That Fit is about more than shoes. It is about self-esteem and children and the future. THAT resonated with me.

What's remarkable to me now is how fulfilling and meaningful my

31

current job is, and also how much I originally overlooked the organization's potential. I had to reframe Shoes That Fit in my own mind to accept the position, and framing the organization in a way that is meaningful to others has been my job for the last seven years.

Chapter 3

What The World Gets Wrong About Nonprofits

There is some good in this world, and it's worth fighting for.

— J.R.R. Tolkien, The Two Towers

Nonprofits play a crucial role in our society, but there are many false assumptions and misunderstandings about the sector and how these organizations operate. Let's start with the sector as a whole. There are more than 1.5 million tax-exempt organizations in the United States (National Center for Charitable Statistics), and recent estimates indicate that about 12.3 million people work in the nonprofit sector. That is roughly 10 percent of the nation's work force—ahead of manufacturing, transportation, construction and finance. (Note: these figures are prior to COVID-19, which is continuing to take a toll on the sector, as well as the people it serves.) Nonprofits are a significant sector of our overall economy.

Americans donate more than any other country in the world. Private donations in the United States represent 1.44% of the country's gross domestic product; that is almost twice as high as Canada, which has the second largest percentage base of donations, followed by the United Kingdom, Korea, Singapore and then Italy. But as a country, the US is unique in the way that nonprofits fit into the broader landscape. As a nation, we have removed government from many "social service" areas, replacing many safety-net service agencies with entities in the private sector. Some of these organizations are for-profit but many more are nonprofit. And while many of these nonprofits work with the financial assistance of government funding, rarely does that assistance foot the entire bill.

There are close to 30 categories of tax-exempt nonprofit organizations defined in the Internal Revenue Code, with the 501(c)3 public benefit charity being by far the largest category. And within the 501(c)3 definition, there are two distinct types of organizations: private foundations and public charities. The latter is what the general population usually thinks of as a "nonprofit" and is the focus of our discussion in this book. Public charities include churches and religious organizations, hospitals and medical research organizations, arts and cultural organizations, higher education and other education organizations, human and social services, environment, animal rights, and other types of organizations to which

Nonprofits makeup 10 percent of the nation's work force—ahead of manufacturing, transportation, construction and finance.

donors can make a tax-deductible donation. Even with the enormous number of nonprofits big and small across the country, most of us in the nonprofit sector feel enormous pressure because there are so many needs that remain unmet, and we care about the people and causes we are serving.

Thriving nonprofits are based on a passion and an entrepreneurial spirit to make a difference in the world. You have to care deeply and creatively to address many of the problems we face. No matter how specific the mission, each nonprofit is part of a larger ecosystem—each specific mission is part of a larger cause. I believe it is vitally important to understand your unique mission as part of a larger picture, and to stay abreast of that larger field.

For Shoes That Fit, our sphere is the intersection of child poverty and education. Our goal is to remove a basic barrier to a child's success by providing an often overlooked necessity—shoes. We connect people with schools that have high levels of need in their own community. The issue of child poverty is overwhelming to most of us, and many of our partners are surprised to learn how much need exists in their own community. When you give people an opportunity to make a difference, people light up. Our message is that everyone can make a difference in a child's life today.

However, there are several myths about nonprofits that can interfere with success. I want to address the two primary misconceptions, which I believe provide the foundation for many misunderstandings about nonprofits, and explain why these they are so disruptive:

Myth #1: Nonprofits should not make a profit.

This myth derives from the misleading name "nonprofit." The name "nonprofit" (or not-for-profit, as some prefer) emphasizes that these businesses do not pass on any of their earnings to shareholders. In the for-profit world, businesses raise money from shareholders who profit off the business if it succeeds. In the nonprofit world, any "profit" is reinvested back into the organization and the social good that is being produced. The IRS tax-code allows donors to take a tax-deduction for donations to nonprofits because of the public good they create. In effect, the word "nonprofit" is a reference to a tax-status. It certainly is not a business model!

Running a nonprofit IS running a business—but you are running more than just a business. You have a double bottom line. Not only does a nonprofit need to have healthy financials to survive (and to receive funding), it needs to create a SOCIAL BENEFIT to society, as well. It is in effect running two businesses. I would argue that thriving nonprofits are some of the best-run businesses around since they have to thrive in not one, but two arenas. In fact, I would argue that many for-profit businesses could learn a great deal from nonprofits. But that's another book. For all these reasons,

I would argue that thriving nonprofits are some of the best-run businesses around since they have to thrive in not one, but two arenas.

I generally prefer the term "social enterprise" over nonprofit, since it focuses on the organization's goals as opposed to its tax-status. But there are many more pressing battles to confront than changing the sector's name. I have a meme on my phone that says, "Pick your battles. That's too many battles—put some back." I need to read that often.

Myth 2: Having low overhead is a good metric for a nonprofit's effectiveness.

I understand the well-intentioned desire to see funding go directly to the people being served. But the reality is that you need to have PEOPLE to do the work of the nonprofit, and they have to have computers and phones and supplies to get the work done. For Shoes That Fit, even if the shoes we receive have been donated, we have to have materials for schools to measure the children's feet, and staff to source and distribute the shoes, storage space and equipment, etc. I think the focus on overhead is a somewhat lazy way of looking for abuse in the sector, but centering it as a key measure of an organization's effectiveness is short-sighted.

Having every dollar go to the cause does not mean that every dollar is used to purchase a shoe. It reminds me of a cartoon I once saw that showed a group of confused-looking pandas sitting in front of a huge pile of money. The sign next to the money had a full thermometer with a sign saying, "Success! We saved the pandas!" The pandas were eating the money. Money in and of itself cannot save pandas. But people use the money to fuel the work needed to protect an endangered species.

A huge percentage of our budget goes to sourcing shoes—over 94% of all funding goes directly to the program in our audited financials. But much has been written about the "overhead myth" and how dangerous it is for nonprofits, so I would urge you NOT to rely on the "overhead" metric in evaluating the effectiveness of a nonprofit. Look at impact—what does that organization accomplish? Is the mission something you believe in? Is the organization accomplishing it? How many people does it help? What is the impact on their lives? What do families it works with say? What do teachers or other trusted sources report? I have said before that I could increase our numbers of children served by dropping off truckloads of shoes in communities. I could purchase cheap shoes, or used shoes. And that might be useful in other situations. But would that accomplish OUR mission?

Nonprofits are indeed businesses, and to have a lasting and continued social impact, you have to have a sustainable bottom line. A healthy financial picture is what enables thriving nonprofits to do their work. You need to invest in employees, the front-line of your work, and compensate them fairly. As flight attendants say, you have to put on your own mask first if you are going to take care of others. Evaluate a nonprofit on its effectiveness in fulfilling its mission.

We always need third parties to fund social enterprises; "self-sufficiency" is another myth.

The Nonprofit Finance Fund has done wonderful work explaining nonprofit finances and helping nonprofits avoid the "starvation cycle" that ultimately dooms so many good organizations. And it starts with understanding that nonprofits actually run TWO businesses, not one.

In traditional business, the value of a product is assessed by the customer, who decides how much they are willing to spend on the particular item. When a company sets the price for a product, it covers the full cost of providing the product AND profit for the business. When you pay $4.15 for a latte, you are paying for a double shot of espresso, steamed milk, a cup lid and sleeve—this accounts for a little more 20% of what you paid. The remainder goes to rent and utilities, labor and profit. The profit margin is either reinvested into business development or goes to stockholders.

Nonprofits do NOT work that way.

For nonprofits, the "customers" we work with cannot pay for our services. So we have to run what NPFF calls a "subsidy" business to cover our costs. Components of a subsidy business can include fundraising, in-kind contributions, investment income, earned income ventures, and "sweat equity" through reliance on volunteers and (much too often) underpaid staff. Because we are not catering to paying customers, we always need third parties to fund social enterprises; "self-sufficiency" is another myth.

To grow an organization's impact and expand its reach, nonprofits need "profits" so they can invest in their own work, improve their infrastructure, and take calculated risks. You will never grow your organization if you cannot make investments in it.

But the goal of the nonprofit is what is so different from traditional business. We need to make money in order to grow the organization SO WE CAN CREATE A SOCIAL BENEFIT! No one is profiting off the income; it is ultimately invested into the organization so that we can reach more children.

Breaking even is never enough.

On Charity and Government Funding

People equate nonprofits and charities as the same thing. This may or may not be true. Most colleges, for example, are nonprofits; I doubt that most of us who support our alma mater consider our donations "charity." The key is that nonprofit organizations are designed for the "public benefit." Public benefit can mean virtually anything—kennel clubs, animal shelters, providing shoes to children, education. You might question how "public" the benefits are, but for a small group of people, that benefit might be particularly important.

A key dividing line in the nonprofit sector is whether the organization receives government funding or not. Government funding is enticing because it can be substantial, but it comes with many requirements and strings attached. In addition, the timing of funding can be unreliable, creating cash flow issues; I have seen reimbursements from the government take up to a year. And funding can vary greatly from year to year, tapering off as administrations and priorities change. The government rarely funds the full costs of programs, requiring the nonprofit to make up the difference; this is commonly referred to as an "unfunded mandate." Finally, the terms of funding can be onerous, often requiring the addition of staff to track expenses and handle the reporting requirements.

Choosing to forgo government funding allows for greater flexibility in programming and the ability to respond quickly to new needs as they arise. There is enormous room for creativity in the nonprofit sector. Even at its best, the government is bureaucratic and can be admittedly slow to address issues. This is not a political observation, but it rather characterizes how the nonprofit sector fits into the broader picture. The private sphere often allows for more immediacy, effectiveness and creativity. As an aside, many Shoes That Fit donors prefer that we work as an independent organization and like our efficiency.

When you become the leader of a social enterprise, you are running a business. Your heart brought you to the mission, but do not fail to recognize what you are everything to organization, and when you are speaking, *Your title says "executive director," but in reality, you are the head of human resources, finances, program development, and the general chief problem solver.*

the organization is speaking. How can so many roles conflate into one person? How do we keep it all together?

There are a number of lessons that I wish I knew before I became the executive director of my organization. Here are the three key lessons that I wish someone had told me at the beginning:

First, running a nonprofit is like being a parent. It is the most demanding job of your life. Like parenthood, nothing completely prepares you for it. Like parenthood, nothing completely prepares you for it. It will give you both sleepless nights and amazing joy. And your voice carries more weight than you imagine.

Second, you will feel like you are in a little boat on a big ocean. The highs are high. The lows are low. Eventually, you begin to build a bigger boat. Remember that rising tides lift all ships.

Third, people are everything. Being a CEO can be lonely, but you cannot succeed alone. You need people you who will listen to you. You need people to listen to. You also need a board that supports you. And you need a staff that is strong, especially in the areas where you are not as adept. If the people you work with feel supported and valued, the organization will thrive.

Running a nonprofit is like being a parent. It is the most demanding job of your life.

Chapter 4

Money, Money, Money

*Remember that the happiest people are not those getting more,
but those giving more.*

— **H. Jackson Brown, Jr**

When I first started working in development at Pomona College, an old friend was excited for me, but then said, "I could never ask people for money!" It seemed unseemly to her. I have heard that a lot over the years.

For me, there are several reasons I feel confident, and comfortable, asking for money. First and most importantly, I am not asking for myself; I am asking for someone else—underserved children who lack basic necessities. Second, I believe in our mission.

And third, I know that people who donate are doing so because they want to make a difference in the world—I am providing an opportunity. I never try to talk people into giving or dissuade them from giving to other causes. I firmly believe there is more than enough money in

People who donate are doing so because they want to make a difference in the world—your organization is providing them an opportunity.

the world. I want to find the people whose eyes light up when they think about making a child smile, who want to invest in our future, who believe that all kids' basic needs should be met. And to find them, you have to ask them. As Wayne Gretzky famously said, "You miss 100 percent of the shots that you don't take."

Donors need to know that they are contributing to something

meaningful, and that you have the means to deliver it. Most people are more conservative in their giving than we realize; donors are asked to fund many causes, and most of us want to be affiliated with success, not failure. That means if an organization launches a campaign for $1,000,000, and I am asked to donate $100, I will probably want to know how much the organization has raised to date. If only a few others are supporting it so far, I have no idea whether or not it is going to succeed. But I do know that my $100 is not going to get it there.

Running a nonprofit often requires fundraising, and fundraising requires momentum. One way to leverage momentum is to build on the relationships that you already have. When a potential donor sees a name they recognize and respect on your website or in your marketing materials, it establishes you as a credible organization. It is like pushing a snowball down a hill—you grow as you pick up more support. Fundraising is about leveraging that momentum.

Because people give to people, establishing relationships with donors is key. When you are dealing with large numbers of people, you need systems to help you manage your relationships. One simple piece of our system is that all our new donors receive a thank-you call from me or another staff member within 48 hours. You truly cannot say thank you enough in fundraising; we want the donor to know that their donation (regardless of amount) is meaningful, and we want them to know that they are part of the Shoes That Fit family. We want to answer any questions they have up front. While people give to people, my ultimate goal is to attach the donor to our organization and cause.

The other key to keeping people involved in the organization is letting them know how their donations (whether of time or money) have impacted the greater cause. We report back. And we use many different media to do this. Our annual report is our "tent pole" publication, telling people how many children we helped during the year, what the impact of that help was, and providing stories directly from the children, schools and donors. But we also share news and stories on social media, by periodic emails and newsletters. And we engage board members and staff in calling periodically to check in with some of our donors.

I am constantly amazed at the number of people I talk to who have their own stories about shoes. A successful businessman teared up when he told me about growing up with holes in his boots and walking to school in the snow. A woman confided about having been teased and bullied at school because kids made fun of her black orthotic shoes. A young couple who saw school kids playing soccer not far from their home with shoes that were falling off. People have their own reasons for supporting your mission, and to truly participate, they want to be heard as well. Learning how your organization relates to the donors' interests can help you stand out from the crowd.

To grow the organization, we decided that we needed to invest in our brand image. In 2017, we were named "Nonprofit of the Year" by the California State Assembly. This was a major vote of confidence by our state assembly member, Chris Holden, and we thought this public vote of confidence could attract more people and businesses to the organization. Of course, we publicized it on our website and with our supporters, but that was preaching to the choir—what needed was a way to get our story out to others who had never heard of us. We were beginning to work with high-profile supporters like Chris Paul, the LA Dodgers, and Gregg Popovich. At the urging of our Nekeda Newell Hall, our Chief Strategy Officer who has a background in marketing, we retained a public relations firm to help us gain media attention from this increased visibility and our distribution events. I knew this was a calculated risk. We negotiated a very reasonable rate with a boutique firm that has taken us on as their charitable partner. In any business, growth requires investment; the decision to work with a PR firm has helped us reach many new partners and help many more children. It turned out to be an enormously wise investment.

Running a nonprofit is a series of calculated risks.

Running a nonprofit is a series of calculated risks.

Fundraising is not easy. It takes an enormous amount of work to engage people in your work, to show them the impact that their investment has made. Success sometimes arrives in a completely different form than you expected. People may see a donation coming from out of the blue and think that it's easy to raise money. But anyone who works in development professionally will tell you the simple truth: those rare, unexpected windfalls only come when you have put in the hard work.

My two favorite stories about fundraising "windfalls" come from Pomona College. I was first hired by Ted Gibbens, one of the "big game hunters," as the heads of college and university development departments were called back in the day. Ted was looking for a director of foundation and corporate relations, for which I had virtually no experience. The committee did not even look at my resume at first. But after a failed search, Ted decided to review the applications one more time, and apparently mine stood out as I made a compelling case even with no experience. He took a chance and hired me. Ted takes credit for my marriage (I met my husband at Pomona) and my career, which he really did launch.

Ted had been both a fundraiser for Harvard and a college president himself before coming to Pomona. He took the job of vice president for development to help the college grow from a regional college into a nationally known liberal arts college. One day, he arrived at his office and saw a letter on his desk saying that a woman he had never heard of had left the school $40 million dollars in her will. He looked the name up in the database and there was no one with her last name there. He was sure it was a joke and circled the office demanding to know who the prankster was.

But it was not a joke.

The *LA Times* headline read "Recluse Leaves $240 Million to Six Institutions" (Oct. 15, 1986). The story reported that "the gifts are the largest bequests most of the institutions have ever received, and will secure the future for some of the smaller recipients, but most were baffled as to why Rains chose them." The family called her bequest an "enigma." Ted eventually learned that the donor, Liliore Green Rains, was a widow with no children but had a nephew who had attended Pomona College. The gift put Pomona on a new footing and was instrumental in its evolution into one of the most renown liberal arts colleges in the nation. And Ted never even met the woman.

The other Pomona story, which I love for many reasons, is about the creation of the "Pomona Plan." In the 1940s, Allen Hawley developed a game-changing concept for fundraising that came to be known as the "Pomona Plan." The college would provide free money management during a person's lifetime in exchange for the donor releasing the money to the college after their death. The donor would receive tax credit at the time of the transfer, receive regular payments for the rest of their lifetime, and know that their funds were supporting the education of future generations after they died. The IRS approved the plan.

But the college leadership was nervous about this new plan. There were concerns that it could divert money away from direct donations. So Hawley was allowed to market the plan to anyone BUT alumni!

This is a story of knowing your cause, listening to what donors want, and not letting anything stop you from making an audacious ask.

Undeterred, he turned to advertising and marketed the plan in the Wall Street Journal. The unconventional plan earned millions of dollars for Pomona College, becoming the first deferred giving program in the nation—plans that are now prevalent throughout higher education and the greater nonprofit world. It also helped spread the name of Pomona College throughout the readership of the WSJ! This is a story of knowing your cause, listening to what donors want, and not letting anything stop you from making an audacious ask. It is the best example of a calculated risk I know.

The core objective of Shoes That Fit is to invest in children's self-esteem by providing them with something they care deeply about that is too expensive for many families to afford: new athletic shoes. To do this, we raise money in a variety of ways. We have developed different programs in response to desires and our own experiences in working with schools, and some of our successes have come out of left field. But it all takes a great deal of work.

Shoes That Fit relies on private sources—individuals, foundations, and businesses—to generate funding from year to year. When I first arrived, we were heavily funded by foundations and businesses, and by one business in particular. Individual giving was the smallest piece of the pie. Knowing that the majority of donations in the US come from individuals (approximately 80%), and fearing our reliance on one particular partner, one of my first tasks was to diversify our funding base.

Corporate partnerships were the key growth strategy being pursued when I arrived, but they were not developing in the way the organization had expected. The ask was for companies to both support the organization financially and also to engage their employees to actually adopt schools as volunteers. We have a number of companies that do each of those things, but very few who do both. So we listened. Companies now have several different possible options when working with us. A business can still adopt schools, encourage employees to buy shoes, and deliver them personally—we have many who continue to do that and have developed deep relationships with the schools they support.

But we learned that many businesses prefer to write a check, but still want to engage their employees—just not the way we were presenting it. While they want to engage their employees in a day of service, the employees do not have the time to shop for shoes in the sizes needed. The companies wanted us to do the work. So we changed our funding request; now businesses (and individuals) can fund the program and show up on the day of the delivery—we do all the work. When talking with new partners, we provide examples of how we have worked in the past, but we start by first asking what their interests are and what capabilities they bring to the table. Then we devise a plan. We are nimble and seek to respond (within reason) to the way that companies want to work with us.

Working with foundations has also been a key component of our funding. For a number of years, this was our biggest source of funding; it is where I cut my teeth in development, and it is an arena I am comfortable in. But the larger, more established foundations do not want to fund organizations' ongoing expenses year after year—they want to invest in helping the organization grow.

They want to help the nonprofit become sustainable. They want to see results. I saw huge potential for Shoes That Fit to ask for larger grants that invest in our infrastructure and allow us to reach more children.

Individual giving is where we have seen the most growth, which is not surprising since it was the smallest piece of our funding pie when I first arrived. And remember, individuals provide the majority of private giving in the United States.

An often overlooked way for smaller nonprofits to increase their base of support is through creating a "bequest" program, asking those donors and volunteers who are devoted to your cause to name the organization in their wills. The appeal of a bequest is that people do not need to give a penny at that moment—and they can donate any amount they like, whether a percentage of their estate or a simple dollar amount. We have developed dozens of bequests in the last few years by simply asking and including the option in our mailings. It is a simple way that people can create a legacy of their own.

One of the key components of our individual giving program is celebrating the results that our donors help achieve. The amount of the check or the hours volunteered—whether a small amount or a large one—is immaterial. Because every ounce of every donation is meaningful to Shoes That Fit, we want to let our supporters and volunteers know how much of an impact they are making on the world.

The message to donors is succinct: our successes are your successes. As an organization, we provide the professional staff to carry out the mission, but the donors are the ones making the difference. When we allows you to listen to the community, learn how they found out about us and what they care about. One of the interesting things I have learned is that many of

Fundraising starts with strategy.

our donors care deeply abou*t* animals,and there is a common thread of protecting the most vulnerable in our society. This resonates deeply with me and our staff. Even in the midst of the pandemic, the amount of funding we received from individuals in 2020 increased over the previous year. Business giving declined, and some foundations put grants on hold or redirected their funding. But people were looking for a way to make a difference, and we provide that opportunity. The need for shoes did not go away. It increased. Jobs were lost, shoes are expensive, and families suffer when they can't meet their children's needs. Individuals have stepped up to make a difference in the lives of our most vulnerable—our children.

When my daughter was born, I decided to take some time out of my career to stay home with her. While spending time with my daughter was important to me, I also began to feel antsy. I was concerned that, when I planned to head back to work, I would feel rusty. Once you take yourself out of the workforce, it can be difficult to get back into it, as many women before me had experienced. My plan was to return to higher education. In order to stay engaged and keep my skills fresh, I found opportunities to consult with nonprofits, at first in higher education but also with some smaller nonprofits. Across the board, nonprofits wanted help with fundraising. But invariably what was needed first was a serious organizational self-assessment. Our work boiled down to several foundational principles:

Fundraising starts with strategy. If you do not have a good plan, it will be hard to succeed. Success is truly a flywheel that picks up speed. You need strategy in place to create success. And strategy starts with crystal-clear articulation of what you are trying to achieve and why. You need to know how your organization fits into the larger picture.

My advice to anyone who wants to start a nonprofit is first not to start one. Scan the landscape for any similar organizations and see if you can work with them. Support them. At a minimum, you will learn from watching how they operate and clarify what it is that you want to add to the equation. Only when you find that there is no other organization filling the need you see, then go for it. But you will have learned a great deal in the meantime that will help you build a strong strategy. People do not want to invest in your nonprofit unless you have a strategy that will be successful.

People want to invest in success. Your track record is important. If people see success, they are much more likely to invest to help you grow. It is much more compelling to show people what their support will accomplish than to ask them to "fill a deficit in our budget." Even if the latter is true, your budget is there to accomplish your mission, so tie your ask to the impact that their investment will make. In my experience, fundraising is like a snowball—it starts small, but as it picks up traction, it gets bigger and bigger. Approach fundraising with goals that are realistic. Success builds on success; the more you raise, the more likely you are to attract larger donations. Make sure you do not forget to share accomplishments. As you grow successfully, your odds of securing more and larger donations increase substantially. While lightning may sometimes strike, reaching skyward to look for a bolt to grab is not a fundraising plan. The hard, very rewarding work of fundraising is found in phone calls, donor meetings, communication materials, celebrating success and the gradual building of a base of support. My goal for all our supporters is to have them see themselves as part of the Shoes That Fit family for life.

It takes time. Starting a nonprofit are "selling" is a vision and a way to achieve it. Donors need to believe you will accomplish what you say you are going to do. It takes time to develop relationships and to earn trust

The hard, very rewarding work of fundraising is found in phone calls, donor meetings, communication materials, celebrating success and the gradual building of a base of support.

from those you are partnering with. It takes time and work to research and identify prospects with whom you share a vision.

Do your homework and be willing to be vulnerable. When the time comes to ask a donor to invest in your organization, you need to know why you are asking this individual, foundation or business. The ask must be specific. This is about building a case. You can never guarantee that someone willmake a donation; you need to be comfortable with silence as you wait for an answer, and you need to be willing to hear no. Do not take it personally; if you have done your homework and made a persuasive case, a no is not necessarily a no forever. Donors have their own timing and plans. Listen.

A Message from One of Our Supporters

Obviously a huge part of working for a nonprofit organization involves fundraising. I'm always surprised by how some nonprofits make it difficult for individual donors to support them. I've had many experiences where I've made a significant donation and then never received a thank you note or acknowledgment of my gift. I have also had the experience of expressing to an university my desire to establish a scholarship in my home state of West Virginia and being met with the response: "we don't have enough students from West Virginia applying to our university to make it worth our time and effort to do outreach there". Honestly, I was dumbfounded by this response because in my mind it would only take a couple phone calls to the local high schools to let them know about the scholarship. And what a great way to encourage students from another state to attend their university. Needless to say, I never set up a scholarship for that university.

My experience has been that when working with other nonprofit organizations I'm often met with resistance to my suggestions or requests and the focus is primarily on getting my money without giving me the courtesy to show gratitude or follow up with regard to how that money is being used. I understand that nonprofit organizations often struggle with mited resources and staff support but if their ultimate goal is to raise support and funds from donors they need to do things that encourage donors to provide those funds and support. Otherwise it becomes a vicious cycle.

I share this information to give context as to why my experience working with Amy Fass and the Shoes that Fit team stand out so much. Not only is Amy Fass one of the most interpersonally warm, engaging, and dynamic individuals I've ever met but she's also incredibly smart, genuine, open and honest. Working with her and Shoes that Fit has without a doubt been one of the most rewarding experiences of my life. They do so many things right when it comes to running a nonprofit and engaging donors.

For starters, a member of the Shoes that Fit staff makes a personal phone call to every donor expressing gratitude for their donation. It doesn't matter how large or how small the donation is, every individual donor receives a personalized phone call. I have received so much feedback from friends and family who have made a donation on my behalf about the impact of receiving this phone call. Often times it's just a voicemail message. The calls probably take less time than generating a form letter and yet have the greatest impact. My guess is the people don't expect it so it's a welcome surprise and it shows genuine thought and gratitude.

Additionally and most importantly, they follow a "yes" philosophy. Whenever I have made a suggestion or request, I have always been met with an open and positive response. Amy will often say "sure we can do that" or "that's an interesting idea let me give it some thought" or "absolutely, I'll take care of that".

When I asked Amy to set up a link on her website for the West Virginia campaign to make it easier for friends and family to support my mission, she did just that. When I suggested partnering with the Clay Center for the Arts and Sciences, she not only responded with enthusiasm she also provided the staff support and resources and came up with creative ways to benefit both organizations and most importantly ensured that children from around the state of West Virginia received shoes. She always listens to my requests and suggestions and thoughtfully finds ways to meet my needs and desires in a way that still maintains the integrity of her organization. Amy also always keeps me informed of how the money I have donated is being used and she always double checks with me before hand to ensure that it's in line with my wishes.

It's not only the fact that Shoes that Fit is a well run organization with a grassroots focus that continuously makes a huge impact and difference in the lives of many children, it's the way in which the organization is run that really stands out.

Thank you.

Courtney Clay Peraza

Chapter 5

Who's Who: The Board and the Executive Director

"None of us is as smart as all of us."
--Ken Blanchard

State laws require every nonprofit corporation to have a board that is legally accountable for the organization's adherence to its mission and its well-being. In fact, the IRS requires a list of board members before they issue 501(c)3 status. In addition to the overall responsibility of the board as a governing body, individual members have three legal obligations, which are often referred to as the "three duties:" the duty of care, the duty of loyalty and the duty of good faith. Simply put, these three duties require board members to provide reasonable oversight of the organization, to ensure that the organization's interests come before their own, and to ensure that the organization pursues its mission. In other words, the board is the steward of the organization's mission. This is very straightforward.

Some organizations have no paid staff and rely on the board and other volunteers to do the organization's work. As the nonprofit grows, most hire an executive director to execute the mission and report to the board. One of the most interesting things about being an executive director is the relationship with your board. The executive director reports to the group as a whole, but they are also expected to lead the organization. This means that the board looks to the executive director for leadership; in effect, the executive director reports to the group they are leading. This is a little less straightforward...

When we have an orientation session for new board members at Shoes That Fit, I often start with a "joke" that I heard from a fellow executive director years ago:

"How many board members does it take to screw in a light-bulb? NONE! The board says, 'Let there be light.' The executive director chooses the best bulbs and delegates their installation to staff. Then the board determines if the light shines brightly enough." This is the most effective illustration I have found to clarify the relationship between the board and staff.

Traditionally, what organizations want from board members has been described as the 3 Ws: work, wealth and wisdom. I want to acknowledge that this simplistic description has come into question in recent years as issues of equity and the importance of including the voices of those you serve at the table have rightly come to the forefront. A number of nonprofit leaders have made a case to end the requirement by foundations and other donors to demonstrate that 100% of board members support the organization financially. The argument is that requiring financial support prevents the board from diversifying, perpetuates capitalist values and does not recognize all the other things that board members contribute to the organization. These are valid considerations, especially understanding the importance of making sure that the people you serve have a place at the table in your organization. Their voices

I believe that clarity in defining what YOUR organization needs from its board is at the heart of organizational governance.

form the foundation of decision-making at the organization. How their voices are heard, as opposed to token representation, will vary from organization to organization.

I believe that clarity in defining what YOUR organization needs from its board is at the heart of organizational governance. There is no simple formula that fits all organizations, and understanding HOW the board contributes to the success of the organization's mission is a discussion that should evolve as the organization evolves. Boards need to address how they contribute to the work, wealth and wisdom at their nonprofit.

For organizations that rely on fundraising (as opposed to earned income government funding or a large endowment) to fulfill their missions, I will make case as to why it is important for board members to make some level of financial commitment to support the organization for several reasons.

The reality for organizations like Shoes That Fit is that fundraising is the organization's lifeblood. It is integral to the mission. For us, our work is to create a "culture of giving" so that we can fulfill our mission. Our mission requires us to connect individuals, corporations and foundations to the need in the community; we require their support. To board members, I would say that it is always easier to ask people to "join you" in supporting the organization if board members have shown that the mission is a priority to them. Many prospective donors want to know the board's level of support because they are assessing how committed you really are. People give out of excitement and commitment to your cause; if fundraising is a priority and those who know the organization best are not supporting it financially, it is reasonable for others to ask why they should.

The number one duty of the board of directors is to hire and oversee the executive director. The day-to-day operation of the organization is the responsibility of the executive director. Building the relationship between the two requires teamwork, primarily between the board chair and the executive director. My firm belief is that, lacking a solid relationship with your board of directors, your life at the helm of a nonprofit will be miserable. What you want are interactive and generative discussions with the board that bring out the best collaborative thinking at a strategic level and avoiding the weeds of the organization. And keeping the board focused rests largely on the shoulders of the executive director, with the support of the board chair.

The reality is that nature abhors a vacuum. Without a clear focus and direction, boards will seek to make decisions about detailed aspects of the nonprofit's work that cross a line into management decisions. This is the land of unhappy executive directors. It can be a frustrating challenge when this is the case. If this happens to you, my advice is to treat your board with patience and respect, but push them gently towards the work that they should be paying attention to. The board's duty is not to make day-to-day decisions or to interfere in staffing decisions. The board does not pick out the lightbulbs.

I am eternally grateful that in my life prior to Shoes That Fit, I worked with a variety of boards, including in support roles as a staff member (at Pomona College and UC Berkeley), as board member and chair, and as a consultant. I have lived on different sides of the aisle, so to speak. I have learned that for a nonprofit to thrive, there needs to be a strong relationship between the board and the executive director. A strong board brings relationships and wisdom to the table that are worth their weight in gold. A weak relationship between the two sucks the life out of an executive director.

For an organization to thrive, the board should not simply be a legal requirement. The goal should be to foster a respectful and collegial relationship that brings the best to your organization. Bringing together a fantastic board of directors with diverse perspectives and experience and creating a common vision for the nonprofit's future will make the organization much stronger. I have enjoyed working with others who can open doors, shed light on situations that are outside my wheelhouse, bring new ideas and share real life wisdom when I have to make difficult decisions, while also having my back.

Throughout the years, I have developed several "rules" for working with your board:

First, for boards to succeed, they need to have a common understanding with staff of what success looks like for the organization and what is necessary to achieve this vision. This is not as easy as it sounds, and it takes work to get there. It starts by grounding conversations in the mission of the organization (in our case, investing in children's self-esteem). While I want the board to see the organization's successes, they also need to understand the challenges we face. Whenever possible, I try to get them to attend a shoe delivery event to experience first-hand the impact of a delivery on children and to learn from the teachers and principals.

Second, you must remain open and transparent with the board. To be successful, I need to know that the board has my back, and they can only do that if they trust me. It is the executive director's duty to provide the board with the best available information; strong decision-making is always premised on good information. Optimal business judgment can only happen when all the decision-makers have access to the same information. Transparency is a key component of success.

The training that the board chair and I invested in together, combined with regular board retreats facilitated by consultants who discuss best practices, was vital to developing a strong and supportive board.

The board I inherited was small and lacked term limits or an agreed-upon giving level. I was fortunate to come on with a new board chair who was extremely supportive. We participated in a training program for executive directors and board chairs funded by the Annenberg Foundation, which was enormously helpful in allowing us to look at the board together and agree on what we wanted to work on. (Our incoming board chair also attended, which made it even more useful.) We had some funding issues, and I was transparent about the financials (the good and the bad), presented concrete plans for fundraising, created committees to do most of the board's substantive work so that members could discuss issues in depth, and worked with the board chair to institute best practices (term limits, attendance expectations, fundraising requirements). The training that the board chair and I invested in together, combined with regular board retreats facilitated by consultants who discuss best practices, was vital to developing a strong and supportive board.

Third, conversation is a two-way street, so take the board's questions and concerns seriously. The board often raises key concerns that you might not have thought of. Sometimes the questions might be uncomfortable. You might disagree. A question that may not seem significant can illuminate an entirely new set of ideas or help avoid previously unforeseen pitfalls.

Finally, invest in relationships with the board. I look for opportunities to spend time with board members, whether in training, board retreats, or in one-on-one meetings. Engaging in relationships can be a struggle for people who are moving quickly and have a strong entrepreneurial make-up. It can be hard to slow down and bring people along with you. I never want to waste board members' valuable time. But I cannot overemphasize the benefits to taking the time to engage with the board members directly. I also try to create opportunities for board members to spend time with each other. I find that some of our best work is done in committee meetings, where there is more time to explore issues in depth. I truly believe that the best board members are made outside of the board room, not in it.

On Underperforming Boards

I would like to offer a word to the wise if your board is not all you want it to be:

- *Get outside help.* It's always hardest to be a prophet in your own hometown. Find a consultant or a well-respected colleague who an offer a training opportunity with your board to explore what the organization needs from the board as it grows, as well as what the board needs from leadership to be engaged and effective. Or attend a more in-depth program with your board leadership. Keep the conversation focused on the mission and the organization, not on personalities. Focus your common vision and look forward.

- *Develop board policies that spell out expectations.* Make everything clear: meeting attendance, committee participation, term limits, fundraising and any personal donation expectations. Whatever you decide for your organization, the board needs to agree to it and then live by it.

- *Be direct.* Board members know when they are not living up to expectations. If attendance is an issue, ask if they will be able to attend "X" number of meetings this year. If not, find out if there is another role that would work more successfully for them in the organization. Board members are volunteers—treat them with respect and understanding.

- *Lean on (or form!) a governance committee.* Whatever you name it, every organization needs a group of the board that is focused on the functioning of the board. Our governance committee reviews agendas, discusses education that the board needs or wants, strategizes annual retreats and other gatherings, discusses onboarding of new members and serves as the vetting group for nominations. When a tough discussion with a board member needs to occur, the governance committee chair (or board chair) should ideally be the ones to address it.

Nothing deflates a group of people more than tolerating poor performance, whether with staff or with volunteers. If your board has performance issues, it is always best to speak with the Board Chair and your executive or governance committee before any damage is done to the board's culture.

Chapter 6

Strategy and Planning

If you don't know where you are going, you'll end up someplace else.

— Yogi Berra,

For nonprofits, discussions around strategic planning can be difficult. In business, strategic planning is defined as a process of documenting and establishing a direction of your business. It helps you determine where you are and where you are going. A strategic plan takes your mission, vision, and values, adds your long-term goals and then outlines the action plans you'll use to reach them. I firmly believe in the importance of being clear about your mission, vision and values, and your long-term goals.

However, nonprofits are not manufacturing a product and looking for a market. We have a service that we are providing, often for the most vulnerable in society, and we are asking a different set of people to fund the work. Our business model is asynchronous. Simply importing a business model into the nonprofit world ignores this important difference.

In his seminal business book *Good to Great*, Jim Collins discusses what he calls the Hedgehog Concept. He chose the term "hedgehog" from an ancient Greek parable: "The fox knows many things, but the hedgehog knows one big thing." The Hedgehog Concept urges companies to define:

    1) what they are deeply passionate about

    2) what they can do better than anyone else in the world and

    3) what best drives their economic engine.

Collins later came to see that many nonprofits excel at the first two, but the third one does not fit. It takes much more than money to make an impact in the nonprofit world—it takes passion, emotional commitment, a variety of talents and ideas. The question is not one of profit but of sustainable impact.

Collins wrote a subsequent monograph titled *Good to Great in the Social Sector* to debunk another myth that he saw: that the "primary path to greatness in the social sectors is to become more like a business." For businesses, financial performance is a great indicator of success. But for many nonprofits, our outputs are inherently unmeasurable. How do you measure a child's self-esteem? His answer is to "rigorously assemble evidence—quantitative or qualitative—to track your progress." For Shoes That Fit, that means tracking the number of children we reach (quantitative) as well as collecting input from the teachers and schools we work with, who report on the improvements they witness in children's lives (qualitative.) And we track it consistently, so that we can see if there are changes in the data trends. The key is knowing what you are tracking. As I have said before, I could easily increase the number of children served if I did not care about the qualitative measurements, which are the key to our program.

The best strategy sessions I have experienced with nonprofits come from becoming crystal clear on their mission, vision and values. The more clarity you have around those—-defining both who you are and who you are NOT—the better strategy the you will develop. Personally, I am more comfortable with the concept of a "strategic framework" than a traditional "strategic plan." The opportunities we need to grab change too rapidly to be led by a series of action steps that were determined years, or even months, ago. But if our mission is clear, if we know WHY we operate the way we do, and what we are NOT willing to do, what we are the very best at and what to leave for someone else, we can make nimble decisions when opportunities arise. For most nonprofits, action plans need to be responsive as well as strategic. Agility and adaptability are two key requirements of most successful nonprofits these days.

Agility and adaptability are two key requirements of most successful nonprofits these days.

Several years ago, the Stanford Social Innovation Review came out with an article entitled "The Strategic Plan Is Dead. Long Live Strategy." The article explained that traditional strategic planning had three components:

1) It used the past as the predictor of future success.

2) It focused on the painstaking process of gathering data that was difficult to come by.

3) It provided directives from the top down since clear communication was unreliable

In today's turbulent world, strategic planning has been turned upside down. The past is no longer a reliable predictor of the future. Data is now easier to acquire, and communication moves at the speed of light.

The article argues for "adaptive strategy" in which experiments replace predictions; pattern recognition replaces exhaustive data collection, and the top-down approach to execution is replaced by ownership by the

As Dwight D. Eisenhower once said, "Strategic plans are worthless, but planning is everything."

whole team. As Dwight D. Eisenhower once said, "Strategic plans are worthless, but planning is everything."

When I was consulting for nonprofits, I was often contacted to create a development plan. Almost invariably, it turned out that what was actually needed was clarity and refinement of mission and strategy. We always started by clearly defining where the nonprofit was: Who do they serve? How and why? What is their "secret sauce?" What makes them unique in their field? If the nonprofit were to disappear, what would be lost?

Then we defined where they wanted to be—and why? If it was not realistic, what was the next step to getting them there? We identified and defined what was getting in the way.

Many organizations begin with a SWOT analysis—identifying and agreeing up on the organizations Strengths, Weaknesses, Opportunities and Threats (SWOT)--is a simple, popular way to begin this discussion. Assessing strengths and weaknesses focuses on the organization's internal capacity, while opportunities and threats analyze your external environment. The key is agreeing on where you are and what you are facing. Outlining your "theory of change" (TOC) is another method; in the TOC, an organization creates a blueprint for the change you are working toward in your community and how your work furthers that goal, as well as what resources, activities and outcomes are needed to be successful.

Often having an external facilitator for these discussions can both keep the conversation focused and help guide through areas where the group disagrees or begins to become stuck. But to me, one of the most valuable aspects to having someone else lead the discussion is that you as the executive director get to listen and participate in the conversation rather than focusing solely on leading the group.

One of the most valuable aspects of having someone else lead the discussion is that you as the executive director get to listen and participate in the conversation rather than focusing solely on leading the group.

Shoes That Fit has built an annual retreat into our board meeting schedule, and we usually have a facilitator for at least part of the retreat so that I can listen as a participant.

The world is changing rapidly. Your job is to keep your organization current so you can fulfill your mission today and for years to come.

Whatever tool you use, the key is having a broad dialogue that includes both board members and staff agreeing upon the basic WHO, WHAT, HOW and WHY of the organization regularly.

The world is changing rapidly. Clarifying and refreshing your strategy regularly keeps the organization relevant and ready to seize opportunities.

Chapter 7

"Culture Eats Strategy for Breakfast"

"It is our choices, Harry, that show what we truly are,
far more than our abilities."

— **J.K. Rowling, Harry Potter**
and the Chamber of Secrets

When I stepped into the executive director position in 2014, Shoes That Fit was entering a new phase of its existence. The focus of the organization was on its reach, diversifying the support base and developing new ways to reach children in need. We sought to increase the number of children we were able to serve. The organization had accomplished a great deal, but some of the strategies for growth were not working. I was convinced that, in order to meet this challenge, we would have to change some of our business practices and staff organization. What I realized inherently but did not know how to voice at first was that we needed to overhaul our culture.

At our first staff meeting, I discussed the values that I thought were imperative to creating a healthy environment that would allow us and the organization to thrive: creating common goals, empowering people to make decisions, creating a "just" environment where we learn from mistakes, support each other and are not ruled by fear.

We made staff meetings more interactive and focused on sharing information. I organized day-long staff retreats where we discussed our common team vision and goals that required us to work together and stretch ourselves. Team-building was key, so we incorporated activities that had us working in groups and having some fun. We also started talking more about what worked and what didn't without judgement; we focused on learning, trying new things and being willing to evaluate our strengths and weaknesses as an organization. People started to be more open. Laughter and food were key.

Looking back, the change took more time than I had imagined. During my first year at Shoes That Fit, I was invited to participate in the year-long Executive Director Leadership Institute (EDLI) run by Executive Service Corps in Los Angeles; the program matched new executive directors with a trained coach for the year and hosted monthly training and discussion sessions for the entire cohort. The experience was enormously helpful.

As an aside, I HIGHLY recommend participating in training programs and spending time with other leaders. One challenge to leading a nonprofit is the constant demand on your time as an executive director. You often feel like all things to all people. You manage the finances, the board, fundraising, human resources, facilities, and everything in between. I think all leaders need to have either a coach or a group of other executives with whom they can speak openly and honestly and receive feedback. It is a great protection against burnout!

I think all leaders need to have either a coach or a group of other executives with whom they can speak openly and honestly and receive feedback. It's a great protection against burnout!

Back to EDLI. The first session of the program focused on assessing your organization's culture. I am a big fan of the late nonprofit guru Peter Drucker, and I have always loved his quote, "Culture eats strategy for breakfast." But as the course continued over the year through nonprofit finances, board development, program assessment, staffing and all the nonprofit issues executive directors

81

address, I realized my discussions with my coach kept returning to the issue of culture raised in that first session. I started to look more deeply at the organization and realized we needed to make some changes. In addition to the positive improvements I was trying to make, I also needed to make some hard decisions.

Change is hard. People are generally hard-wired to fear change. The first thing most of us think (but rarely acknowledge) when we hear

People are generally hard-wired to fear change.

about change is, what does this mean for me? Whether the changes you make are big or small, as a leader, you need to remember how people experience change. While you may think you are just talking off the top of your head, realize that your voice is heard through a bullhorn to others in the organization.

One of the changes that I needed to make was to "unflatten" the staff. When I arrived at Shoes That Fit, there were 7 people on staff, and the other 6 reported to me. As we grew, I knew that would have to change, but I also knew that having people report to someone other than me could be threatening. I did not want to demoralize the staff. Gradually, I began to make key hiring decisions to complement the existing staff members and to work on developing a working-team mentality. The reality is that not everyone liked the decisions I was making. I had to become okay with that. Some staff members, and a few of the original board members, moved on. I realized that was healthy—sometimes people serve their purpose and then need to move on, both for their own sake and for the organization's. Organizations need to grow. Gradually, the team mentality took hold. Competitiveness and fears over favoritism still creep up sometimes, but I recognize it much more quickly and can address it.

You cannot change culture overnight, and it definitely will not change on its own. I know that there are others in leadership positions who have acted much more quickly than I did. Sometimes you have to find your own way. Here are two examples of leadership styles, both heralded as courageous for their decision making, that contrast heavily with my own.

- When former FBI Director Robert Mueller arrived at the US Attorney's Office, he sent an email to 80 attorneys asking each of them to tell him why they should keep their job and what other jobs they were looking at. Perhaps more frightening were the subsequent one-on-one meetings he scheduled with every staff member. This style or approach to leadership sets a tone, conveying authority and clarity of purpose. But instilling fear in employees conflicts with our organization's goals and values.

- In the 1980s, the CEO of an American auto manufacturer was visiting a European auto manufacturer in Germany. The newest model of the European auto manufacturer's vehicle was on the showroom floor, which the American CEO inspected for a moment before heading into a meeting. The American remarked to his German counterpart that his new vehicle's hood had a design element that was notoriously hard to achieve consistently in manufacturing. This new line of cars looked perfect; he wanted to know how they did it. "Simple," exclaimed theGerman CEO. "I fired each group of engineers until they got it done!" While successful, this approach would fly in the face of instilling a collaborative atmosphere to solving problems.

Throughout my career, I have had to become comfortable with my own leadership style and how it influences decisions I make, whether big or small. I tend to follow the Golden Rule when it comes to managing people, and I treat others how I want to be treated. People bloom best when others believe in them. When you are constantly worried about the next step and live in fear, it is nearly impossible to make healthy changes and enjoy your job. No one likes waiting for the "other shoe to drop" (no pun intended).

I have found three things essential in working to change a culture:

- *Ask questions.* I had to listen closely to both the staff and the board to understand where there were issues that needed to be addressed. It takes time and conversation to develop trust that we were all in this together for the same reasons.

- *Develop a solid vision.* People need to understand and be excited about where the organization is going. They need to know how their work contributes to the common goal. We all need to know that we matter.

- *Celebrate small victories.* Vincent Van Gogh said, "Great things are not done by impulse but by a series of small things brought together." We all respond to being acknowledged. It is so important to celebrate victories, big and small.

I eventually promoted two staff members to the position of vice president; I upgraded other titles and as possible made sure annual raises reflected our desire to invest in our people. I wanted people to feel proud to work for Shoes That Fit—proud both of cause and as the organization as an employer. Always invest in your people. They are your best asset.

On Difficult Staff Decisions

Ask any head of an organization about the most challenging aspect of their job. I guarantee they will tell you that letting people go is the hardest decision we make. In the times that I have had to terminate someone, I have spent days banging my head on the wall first, trying to find a better fit, a new role, or a solution. Yet, when we have to concede that there is no solution, there is no avoiding a tough decision. When that happens, the best decision is to part ways. In fact, I have come to realize that releasing an unhappy employee can be the kindest thing to do in the long run.

Chapter 8

Managing Crisis

The way I see it, if you want the rainbow you gotta put up with rain.

—Dolly Parton

Disclaimer: This chapter contains strong language that some might consider offensive—it is not for the faint of heart. But then, neither is running a nonprofit.

One of my mantras in life has been, "Never let a good crisis go to waste." I have said it a lot this year. A crisis is always an opportunity to look at life through a different lens so you can see your blind spots, and to reevaluate priorities and implement change. Humans resist change, which is why sometimes it takes a crisis to shake us up a little.

The first step in navigating through a crisis—whether a drop in funding, an unhappy volunteer, a disgruntled employee, or a PR debacle—is to clearly define the problem. I have had many experiences with organizations that have faced crises, and the core issue is often not what appears on the surface. Start by deciding whether a crisis is truly a crisis. Problems happen all the time. A crisis usually involves a turning-point. Something needs to change.

A crisis usually involves a turning-point. Something needs to change.

If you have sensitive ears, you may want to skip the next section. Blame Stanford Business School and the military for this next topic. It is a framework I have found helpful.

Years ago, I was dealing with a very difficult situation at an organization where I was board chair. In a private session with the executive committee, someone asked when this situation had turned from a "shitshow" to a "clusterfuck." His question lightened the conversation considerably, as no one expected to hear anything like that from this particular person. But the situation, the question and the discussion that followed have stuck with me. So I was surprised when I heard these terms clearly defined in a Stanford Executive Program for Nonprofit Leaders I attended a few years ago.

If you can hang with the language—substitute "fug" for any words that offend you—I find these concepts enormously helpful in classifying crises, not to mention diffusing tension! The terminology comes from the military. With attribution to Stanford Business professor Bob Sutton and author Corinne Purtill, I offer these definitions:

A "fuck-up" is something all of us do every day. We break an egg. It happens.

A "SNAFU" is a military acronym for "situation normal, all fucked up." It refers to the messy state of affairs experienced in many work environments, even healthy ones. Life is messy.

(SNAFU's counter is FUBAR, which is "fucked up beyond all repair." If you are working in a FUBAR, you might want to start looking for other options.)

According to the Oxford English Dictionary, a "shitshow" is a "situation or state of affairs characterized by chaos, confusion, or incompetence."

A "clusterfuck" refers to the actual decision-making process doomed to create a "shitshow." Sutton refers to it as "those debacles and disasters caused by a deadly brew of illusion, impatience, and that afflicts too many decision-makers."

One of our primary goals as nonprofit leaders is to avoid a "clusterfug" at all costs. After much trial and error, here is what I have learned about dealing with crises:

> *"...a deadly brew of*
> ***ILLUSION,***
> ***IMPATIENCE,*** *and*
> ***INCOMPETENCE*** *that*
> *afflicts too many decision-makers."*

- *Clearly define the situation.* Eliminate all illusion by asking tough questions and opening your eyes widely. What exactly is the problem? How serious is it? What is the worst-case scenario? How likely is that to happen? You may change your definition of the situation as you gather information, but clearly defining the problem is key to any good decision making.

- *Never blindside your board.* Ultimately, the board carries the fiduciary responsibility for the organization. Bring in your board chair as soon as possible and decide who else from the board—perhaps the executive committee—should help craft a response or plan. Board members should have the organization's best interests in mind, but remember that they do not know the organization as well as you do—you need to provide the greater context.

- Be explicit. These questions will help you define the scope of the problem and then formulate an appropriate response.

90

A response should always be formulated through the lens of your mission statement.

- *Breathe.* Take time to think through the negative consequences of any action you are contemplating. Consider having a "pre-mortem," where you analyze an action from two different vantage points. First, assume the action succeeded, and then assume it failed. The key to each scenario is to work backward from the end point to determine what actions led to the success or failure. Too often impatience makes the problem worse.

- *Talk to others outside the organization who can help you frame your thoughts.* You want to make sure you are not stuck in a "group think" situation with your board. Reach out to those you trust who have experience in whatever the situation is at hand—that may be an employment attorney, a public relations professional, or others in similar nonprofit work. Your goal is to gain some outside perspective and expertise on the situation. Once again, I encourage you to listen to your gut but check it with your head. This is no time to wing a response.

- *Share bad news honestly and completely.* The worst PR mistake for-profit and nonprofit organizations make time and time again is to let bad news seep out gradually. You want to get ahead of bad news and own it. When it leaks out gradually, no one knows when it will end. This

The worst PR mistake for-profit and nonprofit organizations make time and time again is to let bad news seep out gradually.

91

creates distrust. The only way torestore trust is to be honest and transparent. Do not hide pieces of the truth; as they say in politics, the cover-up is usually worse than the crime.

- *Be willing to be vulnerable.* The current situation may not fall within your wheelhouse of expertise, and the solution you come up with may cause you or others discomfort. Whatever the outcome, recognize your own vulnerability and acknowledge it. Your goal is to create a safe space so that others express their views (especially if the issue involves broader societal issues). Be willing to put yourself out there acknowledging that you do not have all the answers. This is a key component of competence.

- *Pressure test your response.* Once you have listened broadly and feel that you understand the situation and can develop a response, create incremental trial runs of your response. Run it by the full board, staff and others you trust and respect. Staff might feel more comfortable expressing opinions when they are reacting to a concrete response rather than just sharing opinions. Their willingness to improve the message and critique the language is invaluable. This process also helps them own and implement the response. Only after you have "pressure-tested" your response and have buy-in from your key stakeholders should you implement the plan.

As the organization's leader, whether or not you are the "right person" to address the situation is irrelevant. As a white woman, articulating our response to racial justice this last year has been uncomfortable at times.

I did not feel qualified to lead the conversation. But this is not about me—it's about Shoes That Fit and our response as an organization. I recognized that my thoughts inform the organization and how I represent it. That is the balancing act of being a nonprofit leader.

For Shoes That Fit, addressing the societal reckoning of racial injustice and the rise of the Black Lives Matter movement was challenging and uncomfortable. We needed to make a statement. But as with the rest of society, there were voices within the organization that wanted to focus on "all lives." Most of us do not like conflict, especially when it is with people we work with day to day. And as a CEO, it is uncomfortable to disagree with any of your constituents or board members. But I was convinced that the organization needed to make a statement, and I knew that many of the staff were looking to the board to see what the statement would be.

When we firmly embedded our response through the lens of the children we serve—many of whom are black and brown—our position became clear. My task was to create a safe space for our employees and board members to engage respectfully and to address biases honestly. The children in the communities we serve are impacted by structural racism, and we needed to stand with them.

When we are talking about societal issues, we put ourselves in conversations that have conflict. And many of us were raised to avoid conflict.

When we are talking about societal issues, we put ourselves in conversations that have conflict. And many of us were raised to avoid conflict. But the unique moment that our country is facing has been the most serious crisis we have had in recent history. There is too much work to do. People hear the same words differently. As a leader, it was particularly important to create spaces for people to feel respected and heard. I needed to lead the charge on behalf of the organization to do what was right. In the end, I believed that not taking a stand would be a statement in itself.

Confronting racial injustice challenged our organization. But the mission of our organization is to help kids, many of whom grow up experiencing racial injustice in ways they may not even realize. My belief is that if we focus on the kids we serve and their dignity, there is little to argue about. Strategically, it is important to maintain the lens of your organization throughout the experience of a crisis.

Never let a good crisis go to waste.

Chapter 9

The Seven C's

Never let the fear of striking out keep you from playing the game.

—Babe Ruth

The following methodology is a brief summary that will help you and your organization grow to the next level. This framework can be modified to fit your own organization's context, but it draws together the lessons I have learned that have been scattered throughout this book, so I want to address it specifically for you.

Culture

I want to start this section by stepping back to the lesson of my first year at Shoes That Fit—you can have all the ideas and strategies in the world, but "culture eats strategy for breakfast" (and lunch if you aren't careful!). Every organization—every group of people—has a culture that is larger than the sum of the individual parts. Culture evolves, and if it is not nurtured and directed, it can become toxic quite easily.

A healthy culture requires realizing who you are responsible to and what you are accountable for. Who are we serving and how? Are we responding to them or imposing our own ideas? Are we starting in our own backyards, in looking at how we treat each other? Many of us spend as much time at our jobs as we do with our own families; your organization will only thrive if people feel they can bring ideas forward safely and if they can try new things without the fear of failing. Culture and community are a living part of the organization.

Changing or evolving a culture does not happen magically by asking and answering these questions. It only comes by honest dialogue, which requires a safe space to be open. If your colleagues do not feel comfortable bringing forward ideas, concerns, or problems, then you have a culture problem. An organization is only as good as its people. If we as an organization are fractured, we cannot bring our best selves forward to help others. What are the obstacles standing in the way of building a healthy community and culture? The first thing that I do is to sit back and listen, analyze the situation and then take action.

My first staff meeting as executive director (having consulted with the organization previously) was a bit awkward. Rather than focusing on growth goals for the organization, I talked about what it means to be a "just" organization. In a just organization, people are not expected to be perfect—we all make mistakes. The focus is on learning and growing rather than on playing it safe. We encourage people to be honest, and when a genuine problem exists, we bring it forward. Sunlight is the best disinfectant. These were the ground rules that I set down when I arrived, sensing that some staff felt more empowered than others.

I want people who can come to work excited to be there and comfortable being themselves. It is simply too exhausting to try to fit in all the time. No one should live in fear of making a mistake. If you want creative ideas to flourish, people need confidence and to receive honest feedback.

I consider attitude as much as skills when hiring, often more so. Skills can be taught, but attitude is not easy to change. At Shoes That Fit, we have hired people with little nonprofit experience because they bring an energy,

Skills can be taught, but attitude is not easy to change.

vision and drive to think boldly about ways to reach more children. I also make sure that people are supported and respected for bringing their ideas. If something goes wrong, we do not focus on blame—we learn. One of the most important things I can say to any leader is to never throw your staff under the bus. I want our staff to know that I have their backs, just like I want to know that the board has mine.

Clarity

Perhaps no skill is more important for a nonprofit leader than being able to clearly articulate WHAT the organization is working toward and WHY. The more clarity you have around your mission, vision and values, the more effectively you will construct strategy. And the more the community you serve and the people who support the work are aligned with your mission, vision and values, the more successful your organization will be.

The more clarity you have around your mission, vision and values, the more effectively you will construct strategy.

When I think about the Shoes That Fit community, I think about 5 different groups. First, there are the children we are here to serve. We do that by working through schools and teachers, which makes up second group; together the students and schools voices guide how we operate. The Shoes That Fit staff are our eyes and ears on the front lines, and they are usually the first to hear from the kids and schools, so their insight is essential. We also have our front-line volunteers, running programs across the country, and our donors who fund the work. Finally, there is the board. Each has its own focus and culture; but a large part of my job is to make sure that the cultures are aligned around core values—acknowledging the diverse experiences and cultures of those we serve and work with; respecting the expertise of all our partners; listening to others and responding to what we hear; treating children and others with dignity and respect. Our ultimate goal is to have children know that people believe in them.

Our ultimate goal is to have children know that people believe in them.

Connection

The head of any organization has several jobs. They work to create connections between their cause and the community. They need to support the staff to do the great work they were hired for. The head has to inspire the board, empowering them to be ambassadors for the organization. The head also creates a sense of partnership between their donors and those they serve.

Fostering relationships also requires visibility and a willingness to "put yourself out there," regardless of how you feel that day. Investing in your own profile is also an investment in the organization. I spend much of my energy motivating others to explain why our cause is important and our organization is worth their investment. People expect the executive director to tell you exactly why the organization matters. But there is only one you. If you can create a cadre of ambassadors for your organization, your sphere of influence expands exponentially.

There is no special set of skills or a certain personality-type required to lead a nonprofit. But being able to relate to people is a basic quality that essentially builds a bridge between your mission and the donor. Part of relating to others, at least in my case, is letting people know that they can make a difference. People give money to people. The only qualities you need to have is authenticity and trustworthiness. Bring out the best in others, your staff, yourself and donors by becoming a conduit that relates your experience within the organization to the rest of the world.

Communication

To communicate well, you need to hear how you are re being heard. Communication is a two-way street; what you are saying might be perfectly clear to you, but you may be using words that have different meanings to the person you are speaking with. I think there is no better feedback you can get from your co-workers and others than how you and your organization are communicating. Working on your outreach may require the assistance of professionals: hiring a public relations firm, updating your website or wordsmithing with your staff internally on a regular basis. We ask ourselves about our communication and our brand image on a regular basis.

I do not want people to feel bombarded with requests or flooded with information from our organization. We thank more than we ask, and we report back on what we have done with the support we have received. I do not believe you can say thank you too often. Never take your donors for granted. Say thank you, invite them to volunteer, and keep them updated. It is common courtesy to thank someone for a gift. But it is also sound business advice—it so much more expensive to find a new donor than to retain a current one. And there are many major prospects in your donor base, whether you realize it or not. Invest in relationships.

At one of the organizations whose board I was chairing, there was a donor who made donations to us regularly—usually around $10. She was a loyal supporter. She lived extremely modestly, and we all assumed her finances were tight, and her support told us that she really valued what the organization did. Imagine our amazement when we learned that she had left us $100,000 in her will. On the whole, the most generous donors in the US are often those who are the least well-off. Perhaps because they see the need more closely, they donate a larger percentage of their income. Never take a donor for granted.

Many rating agencies require an annual report; we have chosen to use it as our cornerstone marketing piece. Ultimately, I want everyone who reads this report see themselves in it somewhere. This is recognition, either for something they have already done, or something they will do next year.

Cash

To be a sustainable nonprofit, you need to have sustainable cash flow and funding. There is excellent training for non-profit professionals that can aid you in developing financial literacy. You do not need to go to business school, but you do need a basic understanding of accounting and money management. For the organization to thrive, you need to hire good people; to hire good people, you need to pay people a decent wage. You must be able to attract and retain talented people to increase your impact and to grow your organization. And for people to invest in your cause, you need to be a fiscally responsible and stable organization.

Chance

I have given a number of stories about the role of chance in your organization's success. I believe that it is a law of nature that chance does not happen by chance. It happens by hard work and perseverance—it is nature's way of letting you know you are never completely in control. Always keep your mind open to opportunities that come by chance, but keep working your plan.

Be open to taking chances. I call them "calculated risks"—activities that may or may not succeed, but the potential payoff is worth the risk. My conservative nature always asks, "Can I live with myself if this fails?" If the answer is yes, I say try it.

Change

As the Greek philosopher Heraclitus said: "The only thing that is certain in life is change."

Humans like to feel that we are gaining mastery of things we work on. But if anything is clear, the world is changing and—master or not—we must be adept at sensing opportunities and adapting. There are always things to learn. Things often do not go as planned. Life is not simple.

Accept that change is difficult, but it is also an opportunity. Change forces us to open our eyes wider and to notice things we may have been been blind to before. Change brings new opportunities. Listen to your gut, but use your head. When change comes— whether good or unsettling— embrace it. Hold on to your mission, gather information and

Listen to your gut, but use your head.

try to deeply understand what is happening on the ground. Things may not be exactly as they seem to you at first blush.

It is important to have sounding boards—people who are wise, a mentor, a coach, or a group of colleagues can serve as a lens to help you focus and think through changes that may need to happen. Since change is hard, forcing it can be risky. Let time be your best friend. Check your ego to see if you feel the need to make an immediate impression or impact—this can be a mistake. Set your course for change and then approach it in steps. Make sure you have listened thoroughly.

Thinking through the 7 C's has provided a framework for me when I need to make a decision. My goal in publishing this book is to provide a greater context for the role of nonprofits, letting you know that you are not alone, and sharing some of the lessons I have learned with those who may be in similar shoes (pun intended). There will be challenges and crises that you cannot anticipate ahead of time. More often than not, it is nonprofits who step into the gap when the world changes.

Never waste a crisis.

Postscript

Every little thing gonna be alright!

—Bob Marley

I started this book at the very beginning of the pandemic hit. Like most of us, I wasn't sure what this would mean for Shoes That Fit, for our staff, for my daughter in college, for my mother who lives many states away, for my husband and me—for any of us. Shoes That Fit was growing, and we had recently opened a second office, which now sat empty. Schools closed. The whole world seemed to stop, including our funding streams. I was worried.

What didn't stop was the need. It grew. Other nonprofits began reaching out to us. More families were in crisis than ever before. One of the things we heard from food banks was that shoes were the number one item requested after food. Shoes are expensive, and it is hard to live life in the US without them.

The world didn't stop. Los Angeles Unified School District provided more than 100,000,000 meals to students and families. Pomona USD was providing laptops and hotspots for those without Wi-Fi. Teachers were in contact with their students and seeing the needs increase. With the funding we had, we offered shoes. Several teachers cried saying it was the first good news they'd had in months. We stopped measuring kids; we sent size runs with extra shoes to make sure every child got what they needed. Or we let families tell us the sizes. We adapted.

Out of that time came ideas on ways to scale our program. We launched a new partnership with LAUSD, which has long had programs to meet the multitude of their families' needs...but not for shoes. While businesses and some of our volunteer groups had to stop their programs (temporarily, we hope!), individuals and foundations stepped up. We were forced to work on projects that we had not had time for previously, and we even created a new logo with funding by a new donor! With the help of a payroll protection program funding, we ended the year in the black, without furloughing staff and still helping more than 100,000 children.

Our story is far from over. But I am still convinced that adversity is the mother of invention. That people are your best assets. That most of us want to make a difference in the world. That kids are our future.

And that you should never let a crisis go to waste.

—**Amy**

REFERENCES:

Charity Navigator (www.charitynavigator.org)

Council on Foundations

Giving USA

Good to Great and the Social Sector, Jim Colllins (2005)

IRS publication 557

National Council of Nonprofits

Quartz at Work: "The difference between a snafu, a shitshow, and a clusterfuck," Corinne Purtill, Quartz (March 2018, updated Dec. 2019)

Stanford Social Innovation Review: "The Strategic Plan is Dead. Long Live Strategy," Dana O'Donovan and Noah Reimland Flower (Jan. 2013)

The National Center for Charitable Statistics

ABOUT THE AUTHOR

A veteran of nonprofit management and development for over 25 years, Amy's development career began at Pomona College, where she served as Director of Foundation and Corporate Relations; she then worked for the University of California, Berkeley, securing major gifts. After the birth of her daughter in 1999, she began consulting nonprofits on development and strategic planning; her clients included the Claremont School of Theology, the American Academy of Religion (Atlanta), Shoes that Fit, House of Ruth, Inc., and AMOCA (American Museum of Ceramic Art). She has chaired the board of Mt. San Antonio Gardens (retirement community), City of Claremont's Architectural Commission, House of Ruth and Claremont Heritage. Amy Fass was named the Executive Director of Shoes That Fit in February 2014 after stepping in as the interim Development Director; she had previously consulted with the organization on strategic planning and fundraising since 2008.

Amy lives in Claremont with her beloved husband of 26 years Richard. In her free time, she loves spending time with her daughter and extended family, going to Spin and Pilates classes, traveling, reading historic fiction and mysteries, and hanging out with her four-legged family members Rocky and Mila.

Amy earned her B.A. at Stanford University and holds a Master of Divinity from Fuller Theological Seminary. She completed Stanford's Executive Program for Nonprofit Management in 2019.

Made in the USA
Las Vegas, NV
10 March 2022

45410377R00066